JAZZ MASTERS

Benny Goodman

JAZZ MASTERS

Benny Goodman

by Stan Ayeroff

Music Sales America

DISTRIBUTED BY

HAL•LEONARD®
CORPORATION

7777 W. BLUEMOUND RD. P.O. BOX 13819 MILWAUKEE, WI 53213

Cover design by Barbara Hoffman
Cover photo by Lee Tanner

Copyright © 1978 by Consolidated Music Publishers,
Published 1980 by Amsco Publications,
A Division of Music Sales Corporation, New York, NY.

Order No. AM 29307
International Standard Book Number: 0.8256.4201.9

Contents

A Note on the Transcriptions

In this edition all of the solos are transposed specifically for B♭ clarinet. The chord symbols indicating the basic changes are given in the transposed key to relate to the melody line as written. A separate edition (Music for Millions Series 92/040092) is available which contains the same material transcribed for all C (nontransposing) instruments.

Introduction and Notes on the Solos

In writing a book on Benny Goodman I was dealing with a musician who is still active today after more than fifty years in the music business. I have tried to select from his vast recorded output representative selections from each significant period in his long career.

Farewell Blues   October 22, 1931
 Benny Goodman was one of the top studio musicians in New York before he became the leader of his own band. This session was recorded under the name of "Eddie Lang, Joe Venuti, and their All-Star Orchestra." As well as Venuti and Lang this session featured Jack Teagarden who often inspired some of Benny's best work.

King Porter Stomp (I)   July 1, 1935
 A large part of the success of the Benny Goodman Orchestra was due to the simple, swinging arrangements of Fletcher Henderson. "King Porter Stomp," an old Jelly Roll Morton song, was one of the first and most popular and helped to establish the sound and style of the Goodman Band.

Miss Brown to You   July 2, 1935
 A session led by Teddy Wilson, featuring the young Billie Holiday on the vocal. These outstanding first recordings of Billie started the reciprocal recording agreement between Benny and Teddy Wilson, not yet a member of the Goodman organization.

After You've Gone (I)
Who?   July 13, 1935
 With Benny Goodman on clarinet, Teddy Wilson on piano, and Gene Krupa on drums, one of the outstanding small groups in jazz history came into existence. These two songs are both from the first recording session of the Benny Goodman Trio.

Nobody's Sweetheart   April 27, 1936
 Another early Trio recording.

Sing Me a Swing Song   May 27, 1936
 This Hoagy Carmichael tune featured a vocal by Helen Ward, the Goodman Orchestra's first outstanding vocalist.

Down South Camp Meetin' (I)   August 13, 1936
    The Goodman Orchestra in another Fletcher Henderson arrangement
originally composed for his own orchestra in 1935.

Dinah (I)   August 26, 1936
    After jamming with vibraphonist Lionel Hampton at the Paradise Club in
Los Angeles, a new small group was formed. "Dinah" was the second tune
recorded by the Benny Goodman Quartet.

    The next eight songs are airchecks from broadcast recordings of the Band,
Trio, and Quartet on location.

Bugle Call Rag   July 6, 1937
    This is an exciting version of an old New Orleans Rhythm Kings classic.

Down South Camp Meetin' (II)   March 25, 1937
    An aircheck version of the Fletcher Henderson tune.

Peckin'   July 6, 1937
    This was trumpeter Harry James' tune and arrangement named for one
of the routines developed by jitterbug dancers.

King Porter Stomp (II)   July 13, 1937
    An aircheck of this Goodman favorite with an arrangement by Fletcher
Henderson originally made for his own band.

Everybody Loves My Baby   October 19, 1937
    A cooking live performance by the Quartet.

Sugarfoot Stomp (II)   October 21, 1937
    Another great Henderson arrangement which he first introduced back in
the 1920s.

Minnie the Moocher's Wedding Day   April 13, 1937
    Another chart from the old Henderson band's repertoire. With Hender-
son's other arrangements they made up a good deal of the early Goodman
Orchestra's "book."

The Sheik of Araby (I)   September 27, 1938
    Broadcast from the Palace Hotel in San Francisco by the Quartet.

Sugarfoot Stomp (I)   September 6, 1937
    The studio version of this Henderson chart.

Honeysuckle Rose (I)   January 16, 1938
    From the famous 1938 Carnegie Hall concert, this jam session featured
soloists from the bands of both Duke Ellington and Count Basie. Released
on LP twelve years later in 1950, it was the first "live" album to be issued.
The Benny Goodman Carnegie Hall Concert was the most widely sold and
distributed jazz album of its day.

Honeysuckle Rose (II)   November 22, 1939
    Charlie Christian, the first famous electric guitarist, joined the Goodman
organization after having been discovered by critic and producer John Hammond (Benny's brother-in-law) in Oklahoma City. This Fletcher Henderson
arrangement of "Honeysuckle Rose" was one of Charlie's featured numbers
with the Goodman Orchestra.

Dinah (II)   December 16, 1939
    The Benny Goodman Sextet featuring Charlie Christian, another of the
excellent small groups under the leadership of Benny Goodman.

The Sheik of Araby (II)   April 10, 1940
    A studio recording by the Sextet.

The Sheik of Araby (III)   April 12, 1940
    An air check from the Cocoanut Grove in Los Angeles by the Sextet.

I Can't Give You Anything but Love December 19, 1940

This recording by the Benny Goodman Septet included trumpeter Cootie Williams who had left Duke Ellington to play with Benny Goodman for a year.

I've Found a New Baby (I and II) January 15, 1941

Studio recordings by Benny Goodman and his Sextet, featuring Count Basie.

After You've Gone (II) February 4, 1945

This recording (a 78) was from the first session of a later version of the Sextet and featured hot solos by Red Norvo on vibes, Teddy Wilson on piano, and Slam Stewart with one of his *arco* (bowed) bass solos.

Sent for You Yesterday November 9, 1954

A studio version of the old Count Basie-Jimmy Rushing tune by the Goodman Orchestra of 1954.

Let's Dance November 17, 1954

This is a late version of Benny's long-time theme song that was based on Carl Maria von Weber's *Invitation to the Dance.*

After You've Gone (III) September 2, 1960

This version of "After You've Gone" was by the ten-piece band Benny led that developed out of a group started by Red Norvo. The recording is a live performance from Ciro's nightclub in Los Angeles.

For a more thorough biography the reader is encouraged to find the books *The Kingdom of Swing* by Benny Goodman and Irving Kolodin, and *BG—On the Record*, a bio-discography by Dr. Russel Connor and Warren Hicks which lists all of Benny Goodman's recordings through 1969. There are also excellent liner notes on many of the albums.

Stan Ayeroff
Los Angeles, California
April 10, 1979

A Note on Swing

In all of the transcriptions, eighth notes are to be played in a swing manner. This means that two eighth notes  are to be played as the first and third notes of a triplet  .

If the words *straight rhythm* are written above a series of notes, play them without a swing feel (as written).

A Note on Notation

All of the material in this book is written in ¢ or cut time. Since this means there are two beats per measure, wherever possible this division is shown by beaming together all notes within each beat.

Figures which begin with a rest appear with an extended beam.

I encourage the reader to feel the music "in two" from the very beginning. Starting out reading in four will not only make it difficult to play the solos up to tempo, but will also lend an improper feel to the music.

Farewell Blues

Elmer Schoebel
Paul Mares
Leon Rappolo

♩=120 (straight rhythm throughout)

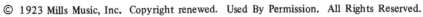

King Porter Stomp (I)

Ferd "Jelly Roll" Morton

♩=96

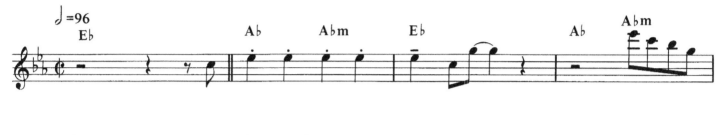

Miss Brown to You

Richard A. Whiting
Ralph Rainger
Leo Robin

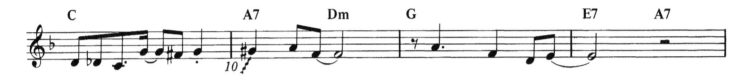

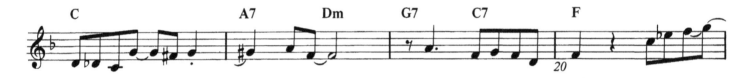

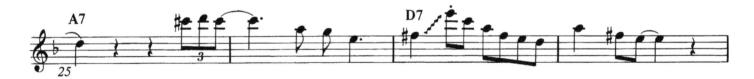

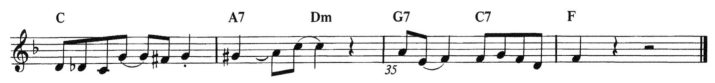

 12

After You've Gone (I)

Henry Creamer
Turner Layton

♩=126

Who?

Jerome Kern
Oscar Hammerstein II

♩ =132 (straight rhythm throughout)

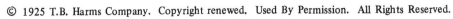

Nobody's Sweetheart

Gus Kahn
Ernie Erdman
Billy Meyers
Elmer Schoebel

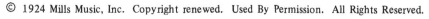

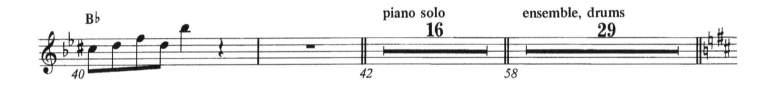

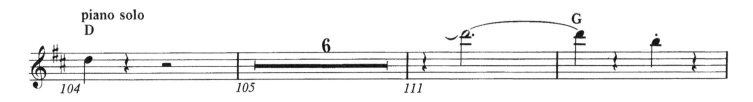

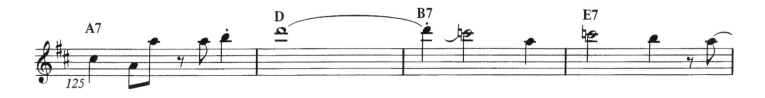

19

Sing Me a Swing Song

Hoagy Carmichael
Stanley Adams

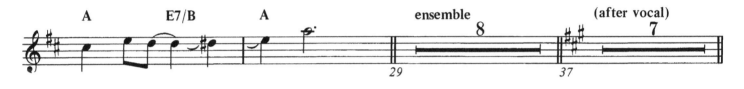

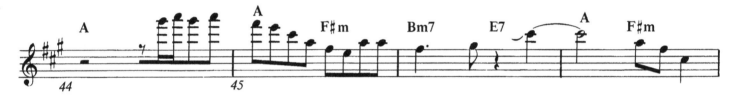

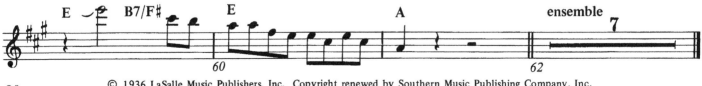

Down South Camp Meetin' (I)

Irving Mills
Fletcher Henderson

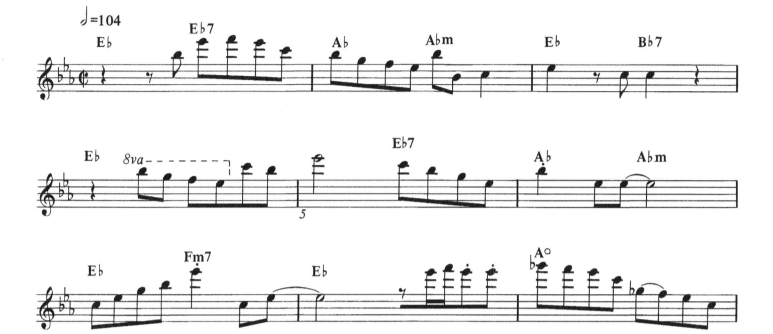

Dinah (**I**)

Sam M. Lewis
Joe Young
Harry Akst

Down South Camp Meetin' (II)

Irving Mills
Fletcher Henderson

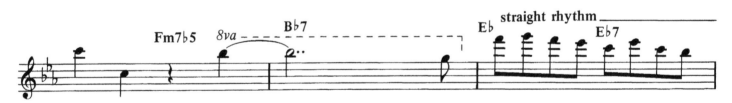

Minnie the Moocher's Wedding Day

Ted Koehler
Harold Arlen

Peckin'

Lew Pollack
Harry James

26

Bugle Call Rag

Jack Pettis
Billy Meyers
Elmer Schoebel

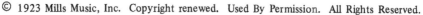

King Porter Stomp (II)

Ferd "Jelly Roll" Morton

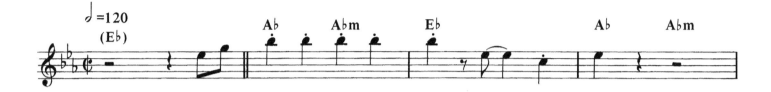

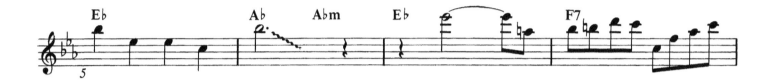

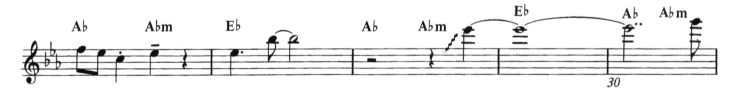

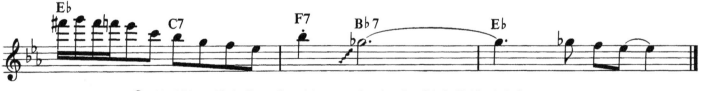

Everybody Loves My Baby

Jack Palmer
Spencer Williams

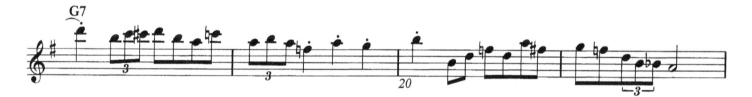

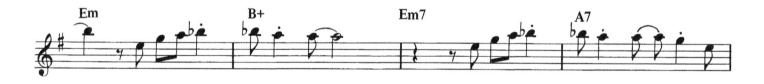

Sugarfoot Stomp (I)

Walter Melrose
Joe Oliver

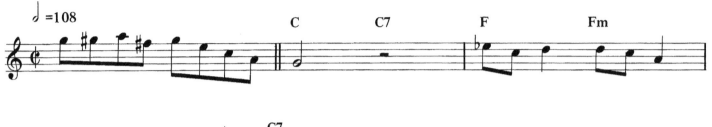

Honeysuckle Rose (I)

Fats Waller
Andy Razaf

31

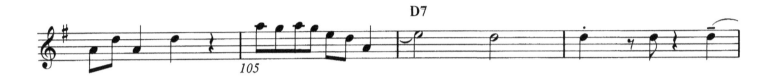

Sugarfoot Stomp (II)

Walter Melrose
Joe Oliver

35

The Sheik of Araby (I)

Harry B. Smith
Francis Wheeler
Ted Snyder

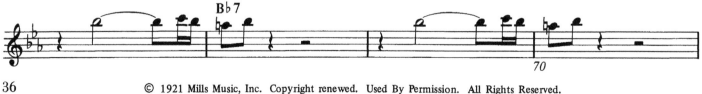

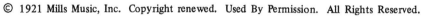

36

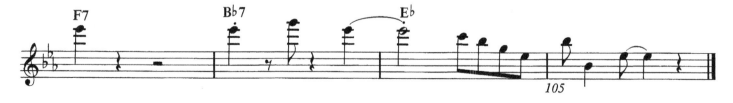

Honeysuckle Rose (II)

Fats Waller
Andy Razaf

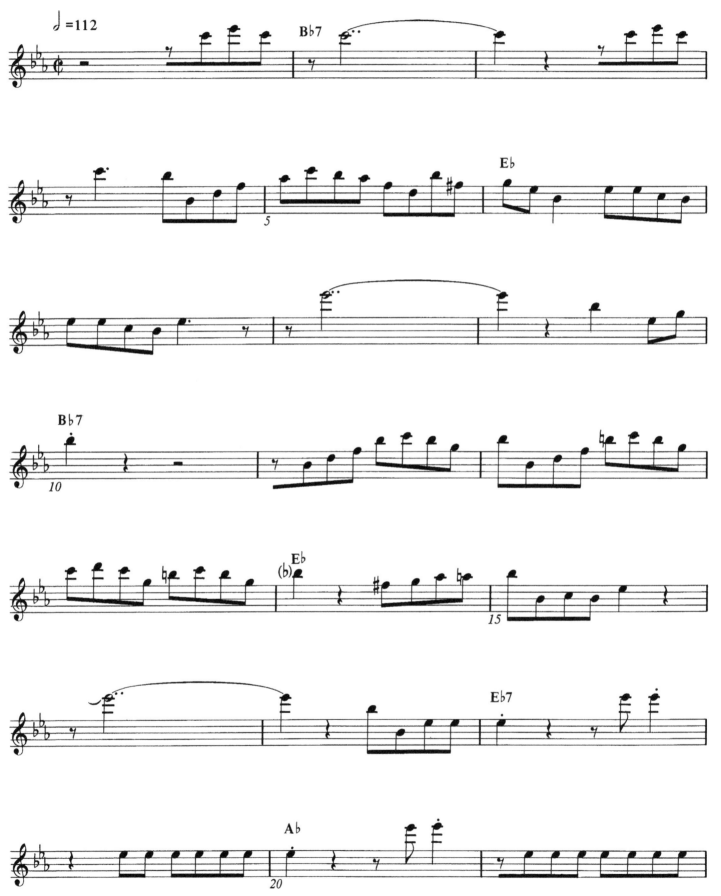

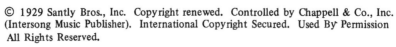

Dinah (II)

Sam M. Lewis
Joe Young
Harry Akst

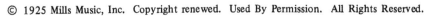

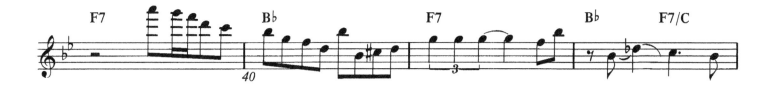

The Sheik of Araby (II)

Harry B. Smith
Francis Wheeler
Ted Snyder

♩=112

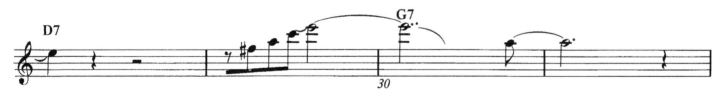

The Sheik of Araby (III)

Harry B. Smith
Francis Wheeler
Ted Snyder

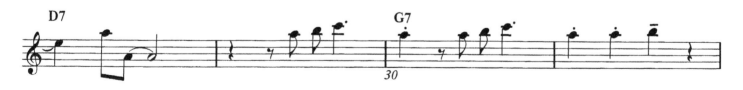

I Can't Give You Anything but Love

Dorothy Fields
Jimmy McHugh

I've Found a New Baby (I)

Jack Palmer
Spencer Williams

I've Found a New Baby (II)

Jack Palmer
Spencer Williams

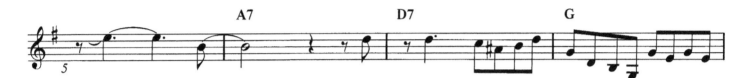

After You've Gone (*II*)

Henry Creamer
Turner Layton

vibes solo

Let's Dance

Gregory Stone
Joseph Bonime
Fanny May Baldridge

49

Sent for You Yesterday and Here You Come Today

Count Basie
Jimmy Rushing
Eddie Durham

After You've Gone (III)

Henry Creamer
Turner Layton

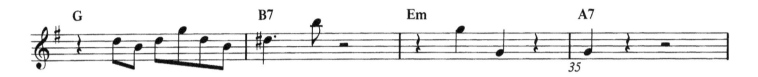

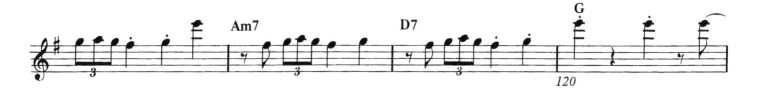

The Benny Goodman Style

Benny Goodman has a brilliant technique that encompasses all registers of the clarinet. He can employ a legitimate classical tone, mellow and warm, or rasp and growl to get funky like the old New Orleans masters. Goodman is a total virtuoso, one who cooks at incredibly fast tempos but is also capable of turning in a subtle and restrained performance as a sensitive interpreter of a ballad.

I call the early jazz style of the 1920s and 1930s "ornamented arpeggio." This means that most of the notes are chosen from chord tones, while using various contrapuntal devices to lend interest to the melodic line. Rather than just run through the chord tones, Goodman always plays a melodic idea or motif that is often developed over many measures.

His solos include liberal use of ninth, eleventh, and thirteenth chords as well as their alterations (flat fifth, sharp fifth, flat ninth, and sharp ninth). Rhythmic drive is frequently accomplished by anticipating the next chord change on the last beat of a measure.

The style of this period is also highly chromatic. The following chart shows how it is possible to use all twelve tones of the chromatic scale.

The Chromatic Scale
Functions of each scale degree as related to a C chord:

C	root (chord tone)
C♯ /D♭	chromatic passing tone between root and ninth
D♭	flat ninth (chord tone)
D	ninth (chord tone); also functions as a second, a scalewise passing tone between root and third
D♯ /E♭	chromatic passing tone between ninth and tenth
E♭	flat third (blues note); also chord tone in minor chord
E	third (chord tone)
F	appoggiatura fourth, usually followed by sharp second to third; also scalewise passing tone between third and fifth
F♯ /G♭	chromatic passing tone (when preceded by fourth) between third and fifth (e.g. E F F♯ G)
G♭	flat fifth (blues note)
G	fifth (chord tone)
G♯ /A♭	chromatic passing tone between fifth and sixth
G♯	sharp fifth (altered chord tone)
A	sixth (chord tone); sometimes grace note to flat seventh
B♭	flat seventh (blues note)
B	major seventh (chord tone in major seventh chord); sometimes grace note to root
C♭	chromatic passing tone between root and flat seventh

The following excerpts illustrate some of the concepts used throughout the transcribed solos in this book. Though it is the aim of this analysis to give the reader a greater understanding of the music of Benny Goodman, it should be kept in mind that there will always be things which are difficult to explain. Some notes do not fit easily into a category, yet they work. It is these exceptions, the reaching for new ideas, that mark the supreme soloists.

First, a word about connecting chord tones:

1. *Chord Tone to Chord Tone* (R, 3, 5, etc.)
   Simply play an arpeggio, or go from a chord tone of one chord to a chord tone of another chord.
2. *Passing Tones* (PT)
   A. Scalewise: Fill in the notes of the scale between chord tones.
   B. Chromatic: Fill in the notes of the chromatic scale between chord tones.
3. *Ornaments*
   A. Auxiliary tones (AUX): Play a note, a half or a whole step above or below a chord tone, then return to the chord tone. (The chord tone needn't always be played first.)
   B. *Surrounding Note Figure* (SNF): Play a combination of half step below and then one scale step above any chord tone–starting either above or below the chord tone.

Benny Goodman always knows where the melodic line is going. He has such amazing chops that he can be creative and yet relaxed at "killer-diller" tempos which would scare a lesser player. His rhythmic drive is frequently accomplished by anticipation of the next chord change on the last beat of a measure. This is marked ANT in the excerpts.

A final note: Benny often uses octave leaps (OCT) in the following melodic lines.

This is the first bridge to "Honeysuckle Rose" (I). Most chord structures of this period are based on the circle of fifths, of V-to-I progressions. The sequence in this excerpt is G7 (V of C) to C (I) to A7 (V of D) to D7 (V of G). This passage shows chord tones, octave leaps, scalewise and chromatic passing tones, and the surrounding note figure. Notice the development of the idea starting in measure 6, continuing to measure 7.

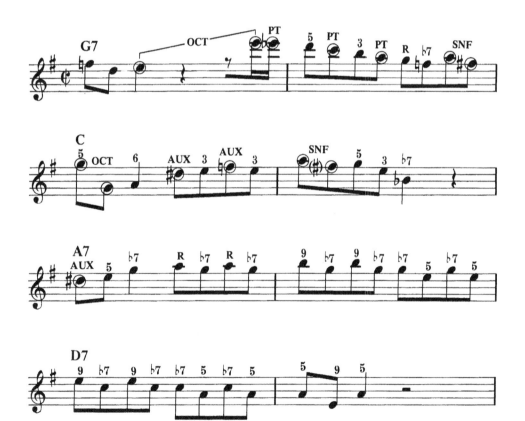

This is the third bridge to "Honeysuckle Rose" (I), illustrating the use of the auxiliary tone as a melodic motif in measures 1 and 2.

This is a bridge from "Honeysuckle Rose" (II), further illustrating the concepts discussed previously.

This is the second half of the chorus on "After You've Gone" (II). It is taken at the breakneck tempo ♩=**160**. Note the simple arpeggio that starts it in measures 1 through 4; it's like an exercise, but very effective when played at such a fast tempo. Benny really had it under his fingers, so to speak. Notice the anticipation on measure 24 which really drives into the tonic G chord to end an exciting chorus.

Now go to the source and listen to the records themselves to capture what isn't on paper—the phrasing and tonal nuances which have made Benny Goodman a jazz master for over 50 years.

Discography

The following is a discography of the transcribed solos of Benny Goodman that appear in this book. Some albums are imports and some are out of print. Either write the record company or look in the vintage jazz section of your nearest major record store (or one that specializes in rare and out-of-print jazz albums).

The Golden Horn of Jack Teagarden
MCA 227
"Farewell Blues"

This is Benny Goodman
RCA VPM6040
"King Porter Stomp" (I), "Down South Camp Meetin' " (I), "Sugarfoot Stomp" (II)

The Complete Benny Goodman Vol. 1—1935
RCA Bluebird AXM2-5505
"King Porter Stomp" (I), "After You've Gone" (I), "Who?"

Lady Day—Billie Holiday
Columbia CL637 The Golden Era Series
"Miss Brown to You"

Billie Holiday's Greatest Hits
Columbia CL2666
"Miss Brown to You"

Billie Holiday—The Original Recordings
Columbia C32060
"Miss Brown to You"

The Complete Benny Goodman Vol. 3—1936
RCA Bluebird AXM2-5532
"Down South Camp Meetin' " (I), "Dinah" (I)

Benny Goodman Trio & Quartet (1935-1938)
RCA 730.629 Black & White Vol. 18
"After You've Gone"(I), "Who?," "Dinah" (I)

B.G.: The Small Groups/Benny Goodman
RCA Vintage Series LPV521
"Nobody's Sweetheart"

Benny Goodman Trio et Quartet Vol. 2
RCA 730707 Black & White Vol. 27
"Nobody's Sweetheart"

The Complete Benny Goodman Vol. 2—1935-1936
RCA Bluebird AXM2-5515
"Sing Me a Swing Song"

The King of Swing Benny Goodman: Complete 1937-1938 Jazz Concert no.2
Columbia OSL180
"Bugle Call Rag," "Down South Camp Meetin' "(II), "Peckin'," "King Porter Stomp" (II), "Sugarfoot Stomp" (II), "Everybody Loves My Baby," "Minnie the Moocher's Wedding Day," "The Sheik of Araby" (I)

Benny Goodman Carnegie Hall Jazz Concert
Columbia OSL160
"Honeysuckle Rose" (I)

Solo Flight The Genius of Charlie Christian
Columbia CG30779 The John Hammond Collection
"Honeysuckle Rose" (II), "I Can't Give You Anything but Love," "I've
Found a New Baby" (II)

Charlie Christian Live 1939/1941
Jazz Anthology Musiodisc 30JA5181
"Dinah" (II), "The Sheik of Araby" (III)

Charlie Christian with the Benny Goodman Sextet, Septet & Orchestra
CBS 62581 Aimez Vous le Jazz no. 3
"The Sheik of Araby" (II), "I've Found a New Baby" (I), "I Can't Give You
Anything but Love," "Honeysuckle Rose" (II)

Benny Goodman Sextet
Columbia 33817 (This is a 78 rpm recording not issued on LP.)
"After You've Gone" (II)

The Hits of Benny Goodman
Capitol SM1514
"Sent For You Yesterday and Here You Come Today,"
"Let's Dance"

Benny Swings Again
Columbia CL1579
"After You've Gone" (III)